FROGS

Written and edited by **Lucy Baker**

Consultant Vic Taylor, Education Officer,
British Herpetological Society, London

TWO-CAN

First published in Great Britain in 1991 by
Two-Can Publishing Ltd
27 Cowper Street
London EC2A 4AP

© Two-Can Publishing Ltd, 1991

© Text by Lucy Baker, 1991
Typesetting by The Creative Text Partnership
Printed in Italy by Amadeus – Rome

All rights reserved. No part of this publication may be reproduced, stored in a retrieval system, or transmitted in any form or by any means, electronic, mechanical, photocopying, recording or otherwise, without prior written permission of the copyright owner.
The JUMP! logo and the word JUMP! are registered trade marks.

British Library Cataloguing in Publication Data
Baker, Lucy
Frogs.
1. Frogs
I. Title
597.89

ISBN 1-85434-089-1

Photographic Credits:
Front Cover Bruce Coleman p.4 Francois Gohier/Ardea p.5 Pat Morris/Ardea p.6-7 John Daniels/Ardea p.8 Hans and Judy Beste/Ardea p.9 (top) Annie Price/Survival Anglia (bottom) Bruce Davidson/Survival Anglia p.10-11 Des and Jen Bartlett/Survival Anglia p.12 George McCarthy/Bruce Coleman p.14 Avril Ramage/Oxford Scientific Films p.15 (top) Zig Leszczynski/Animals/Animals/Oxford Scientific Films (bottom) Ken Griffiths/NHPA p.16 G I Bernard/Oxford Scientific Films p.17 Michael Fogden/Oxford Scientific Films p.18 Michael Leach/NHPA p.19 Heather Angel

Illustration Credits:
Back Cover p.4-19 David Cook/Linden Artists p.20-21 Steve Ling/Linden Artists p.22-23 Claire Legemah p.24-25 Ken Hooks/Jeremy Clegg p.26-30 Phil Weare/Linden Artists p.31 Alan Rogers

CONTENTS

Looking at frogs	4
On the move	6
Homes for frogs	8
Mating time	10
Taking shape	12
Food for frogs	14
Staying alive	16
Frogs and people	18
Pond game	20
Frog mask	22
Find the frogs	24
The dry desert frogs	26
True or false?	31
Index	32

LOOKING AT FROGS

Frogs belong to an ancient group of animals called amphibians. Other members of the group include newts and salamanders. Amphibians have been on this earth far longer than reptiles, birds and mammals. When they first appeared, over 300 million years ago, the only creatures that lived on land were insects and other creepy crawlies.

Most frogs begin life in water but spend their adult life on land. They return to freshwater ponds and streams each year to mate.

There are over 1,800 different kinds of frog. Typically, a frog has a short, round body, long back legs and shorter front legs. Most frogs have large bulbous eyes that rise above the level of their head.

Frogs have soft, delicate skin that is kept moist by special mucous glands. Some frogs appear wet and slippery, while others look dry and warty.

Toads are members of the frog family. Usually, toads are recognised by their dry, warty skin but in some parts of the world there are smooth-skinned toads and warty-skinned frogs.

▶ The White's tree frog is round and fat. It measures up to ten centimetres (four inches). The largest frogs can be three times that size.

▼ Not all frogs are fat. The red-eyed tree frog is thin and angular. It lives in the rainforest trees of Central America.

ON THE MOVE

Frogs are champion jumpers. By pushing off the ground with their long back legs, they can travel many times their body length in a single leap. Frogs soften the impact of landing with their stocky front legs.

Generally frogs can jump further than toads because their legs are longer. In some parts of the world, yearly contests are held to find the frog that can jump the furthest.

Besides jumping, frogs can also move on all fours. They have strong toes which they use to grip on to twigs, stones and other useful footholds when they are climbing up trees or over rocky ground. Frogs are also good at digging into the ground.

Not surprisingly, frogs are just as capable in water as they are on land. To swim, they use their powerful back legs to push themselves along and steer with their front legs. Most frogs have webbed or partly webbed feet.

When seated, frogs tuck their long back legs under their body. The frog in this picture is the European frog.

INDEX

African bullfrog 9,10
African horned frog 15
amphibians 4
arrow poison frog 18,19

breathing 9
bullfrog 9,10,18

clawed frog 14
communication 9,17

defence 16,17
diet 14

eggs 10,11,12,13
enemies 16,17
European frog 6
European toad 14,16

feet 6

golden bell frog 9
great grey tree frog 11
green tree frog 15

habitats 8

jumping 6

marsupial tree frog 11
mating 10,11
metamorphosis 12
midwife toad 11
movement 6,7

narrow-mouthed frog 14

oriental fire-bellied toad 17

poisonous frogs 16,18
problems 18

red-eyed tree frog 4

size 4
skin 4
sloughing 12
spawn 12
swimming 6

tadpoles 12
toads 4
toes 6,8
tree frogs 4,5,8,11,15

White's tree frog 5

TRUE OR FALSE?

Which of these facts are true and which ones are false? If you have read this book carefully you will know the answers.

1. Frogs belong to an ancient group of animals called amphibians.
2. Frogs begin life on land but live their adult life in water.

3. Frogs have short back legs and long front legs.
4. Frogs have small, deep-set eyes.
5. Toads are members of the frog family.
6. Frogs have strong toes.

7. Frogs are noisiest during their breeding season.

8. Most frogs live on the frozen landmass called Antarctica.
9. Bullfrogs make a loud, bellowing noise.
10. Baby frogs are called tadpoles.
11. Tadpoles look just like miniature frogs.
12. Frogs eat plants.

13. Some frogs have poisonous skin.
14. Some people eat frogs' legs as a delicacy.
15. Some poisonous frogs are called arrow poison frogs.

Answers: 1. True; 2. False; 3. False; 4. False; 5. True; 6. True; 7. True; 8. False; 9. True; 10. True; 11. False; 12. False; 13. True; 14. True; 15. True.

The eggs will grow incredibly quickly. They will hatch after just 24 hours and the tadpoles that emerge will change into toads in less than two weeks. All the time they are growing, the tadpoles' freshwater home will be shrinking as the hot desert sun evaporates the water.

Only a few of the thousands of eggs laid will survive. Competition is fierce. The smallest, weakest tadpoles will be eaten by the other tadpoles in the pond, or by other desert creatures looking for food.

The mating race leaves Sam hungry and tired. Now, he has only a few hours to look for food before the sun rises again and forces him underground.

However, rains bless the Sonoran Desert. They change the empty hostile land into a colourful garden. For a few weeks, flowers bloom and insects and butterflies fill the air. It is a magic transformation.

Although Sam cannot roam freely during the day, each night he can venture out and have his fill. That is, until the desert becomes dry and hostile again.

For a few weeks Sam's life revolves around feasting and glorious freedom. He picks spiders, grasshoppers and caterpillars from the flowers to build up his fat reserves. He must eat a huge amount of food to prepare for the dry months ahead.

All too soon the ground dries up. Sam and his friends are forced to bury themselves deep below the desert floor. A few new toads will be joining them. They have only just begun their desert life.

New spadefoot toads would never survive if Sam and his friends did not scurry to the temporary mating pools as soon as they had emerged. The shallow puddles of water where the female toads must lay their eggs will only be around for a few weeks. This is the most important event in the toads' lives. There is no time to stop to eat because there is not enough room in the water for every toad, so Sam hurries to the ponds with the others.

As Sam nears the pool, he can hear the harsh cries of the male toads. These are mating calls to the females, and each toad tries to be louder than his rivals. Sam adds his voice, inflating his throat like a balloon to give his call. Sam is lucky. He squeezes into the pond and finds a partner. In one single night he will fertilise hundreds of her eggs.

floor. In a few hours, temporary pools will have formed where the toads can gather to mate.

Spadefoot toads are very lucky because they have a sort of sixth sense. They can tell whether it is night or day from their underground homes. If the rains fall in the daytime, as they often do, the toads wait patiently for the sun to set before they struggle up to the surface. Even after a rare rainstorm, the desert sun is too fierce for them to face.

At last, the sun drops from the sky and Sam and the other toads begin to stir. Although they cannot see or hear one another, they move together. Within minutes, the still and empty desert floor erupts and hundreds upon hundreds of toads spill out over the wet ground.

Sam is tempted to search for food as soon as he breathes the cool night air. He has not eaten for months. But he must first join in a scramble for the survival of his species.

sun would take all the moisture from his body and, within a few hours, he would be dead.

To survive, Sam remains deep underground. He has a horny plate — a spade — on each hind foot to dig himself into the soil. It is much cooler beneath the surface of the desert.

Unbelievable though it may seem, Sam has to live underground for ten months at a time. Buried alive, he does as little as possible. He falls into a special kind of sleep, like other animals that hibernate through cold winter months.

Sam's favourite time of the year is when rains fall on the Sonoran Desert. These rains are not just light showers, they are torrential downpours.

The drumming desert rains wake Sam from his deep sleep like an alarm clock. They make a thundering noise on the ceiling of his burrow. Sam is not the only spadefoot toad woken by the rainfall. All his friends hear the drumming noise too.

The desert toads are happy and relieved. They know the pounding rains promise a chance to eat and that the rush of water will flood the desert

THE DRY DESERT FROGS

BY LUCY BAKER

Sam is a spadefoot toad. Like his mother and father and other spadefoot toads, he lives in a desert. It is not the easiest place for a frog to live.

Sam's desert is the Sonoran Desert, in Arizona, USA. It is a very hot, very dry place. Rain, if it falls at all, can only be expected two months of the year.

Most of the time, a blazing sun bakes the Sonoran Desert. By midday it is hot enough to fry an egg on the desert floor. There are no trees, only spiky cacti and mean-looking succulents.

If Sam ventured up to the desert surface during the long, hot days, he would be in terrible danger. The cruel

FROG MASK

There are lots of ways to decorate masks. Here are a few things to try.

crayons   string

paint

fabric

coloured paper

Try making a mask. You will need a piece of cardboard or thick paper, a length of elastic or string and a pair of scissors.

Draw and carefully cut out the basic mask shape. Remember to make two small holes for your eyes and a small hole at each side of the mask. Decorate your mask and then thread the piece of elastic or string through the holes at the sides.

Now your mask is ready to wear!

▶ Our mask was made by cutting out this basic shape from cardboard and covering it with paper shapes.

FROGS AND PEOPLE

Over the years, people have been very suspicious of frogs. They have associated them with witchcraft and sorcery. The appearance of frogs in large numbers during the breeding seasons was the source of folk tales about them raining from the skies.

Frogs do us no harm. In fact, they are our friends because they eat harmful pests. In some parts of Asia, people have hunted frogs in very large numbers and now plagues of insects threaten their farmers' crops.

The growing number of people has caused many problems for frogs. Their homes are disappearing as natural habitats are replaced by roads and buildings. Man-made pollutants, that are now regularly washed into rivers and streams, poison the frogs' spawning grounds.

FROGS TODAY

In some countries, road signs are displayed to try and protect frogs during their annual migration to breeding grounds.

Some people eat frogs. Bullfrogs are bred for their long back legs, which are sold as a delicacy all over the world.

◀ Every year, frogs and toads are killed on the way to their mating grounds. They always follow the same route, even if it means crossing dangerous fast roads.

▶ Some poisonous frogs are called arrow poison frogs because their poison is used by rainforest tribes to tip their hunting arrows. Even though most arrow poison frogs are no bigger than a human fingertip, their poison can kill large animals like wild cats.

◀ The European toad makes itself look as big as possible when it is threatened by snakes, lizards or other familiar enemies. It stands on all fours and puffs up its body.

▲ The oriental fire-bellied toad shows its brightly coloured belly to attackers. The red, orange or yellow pattern warns of poisons produced under the toad's skin.

DEFENCE FACTS

The casque-headed frog's angular features and mottled skin give it perfect camouflage in its leaf litter home.

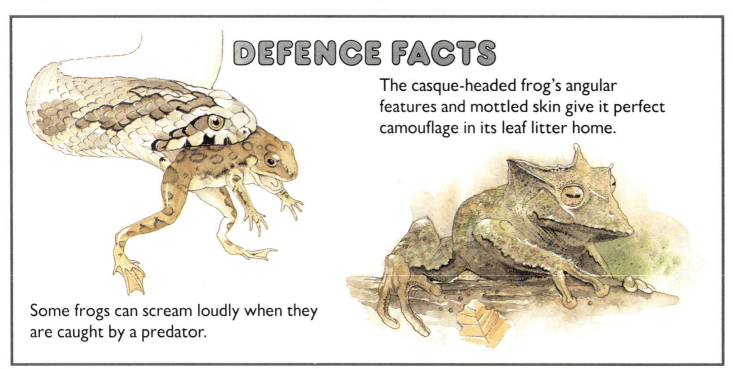

Some frogs can scream loudly when they are caught by a predator.

STAYING ALIVE

A frog's life is fraught with danger from the start. Most tadpoles do not survive long enough to become frogs. They are picked off by fish, birds and each other before they leave the water.

Adult frogs have just as many enemies. They must keep a constant look-out for predators. Reptiles, birds and many mammals eat frogs as part of their diet.

Many frogs are a mottled green or brown. The colour of their skin blends in with their natural surroundings making them difficult to spot.

If they are in danger, frogs have a number of different ways of trying to escape. Many frogs flee from their predators by hopping away or burrowing into the ground. A few frogs puff themselves up or rise on all fours to challenge their attackers.

The best protection a frog can have is a poisonous skin. Any animal foolish enough to sample a poisonous frog quickly learns its lesson because chemicals made under the frog's skin cause painful swellings in the attacker's mouth. Poisonous frogs have bold, bright markings to warn other animals to stay away.

▲ A full sized mouse is no problem for the African horned frog. Most large frogs can push their eyes out of their sockets to make the mouth cavity bigger.

▶ Some frogs will leap into the air to bring down dragonflies, moths and other flying insects. Others will shoot them down with their long, sticky tongue. This green tree frog is eating a moth it has just caught.

FOOD FOR FROGS

All frogs are carnivores. This means they eat animals rather than plants. Frogs will eat almost anything that moves. They spend much of their time sitting very still so that they can catch small creatures as they pass by. Their big, bulging eyes give them good all-round vision and they are quick to react to movement.

Most frogs live on a diet of insects, worms and grubs but larger frogs, like horned frogs and bullfrogs, eat lizards, birds and other small animals.

Some frogs have a long, sticky tongue attached to the front of their mouth. When they see something tasty, they shoot it down with their high-speed tongue. Other frogs simply grab at crawling insects with their strong, wide jaws.

The clawed frog, which spends its entire life in water, scoops food into its mouth with its front legs. Narrow-mouthed frogs have such small mouths that their diet is restricted. They can only pick termites and other tiny creatures from the ground.

▼ Worms are easy pickings for frogs like the European toad. Frogs clean worms with their feet before putting them into their mouths.

TAKING SHAPE

Frogs' eggs can take anything from a few days to a few weeks to hatch, depending on the weather. Tiny animals emerge that look more like fish than frogs. These creatures are called tadpoles.

Tadpoles have to go through many changes before they become young frogs. At first, they live like small fish. They breathe through gills and eat tiny water plants called algae.

The first change comes when tadpoles develop lungs and begin to breathe at the surface of the water. Around the same time, their diet changes from plants to animal products. A short while later, tiny limbs grow out of the tadpoles' bodies.

By the time most tadpoles are three months old, they are ready to leave the water and hop about on land. At last, they are tiny replicas of their parents. When animals change their shape — as tadpoles do to become frogs — it is called metamorphosis.

Most frogs continue to grow for about three years before they reach full adult size. Frogs regularly shed the outermost layer of their skin as they grow. This skin-shedding process is called sloughing.

▶ Frogs' eggs are called spawn. Frog spawn usually floats in huge clusters on the surface of the water whereas toad spawn is laid in strings and wrapped around underwater plants.

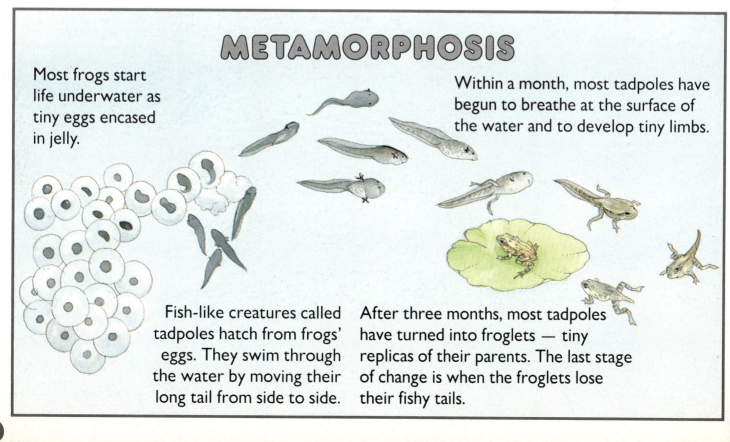

METAMORPHOSIS

Most frogs start life underwater as tiny eggs encased in jelly.

Fish-like creatures called tadpoles hatch from frogs' eggs. They swim through the water by moving their long tail from side to side.

Within a month, most tadpoles have begun to breathe at the surface of the water and to develop tiny limbs.

After three months, most tadpoles have turned into froglets — tiny replicas of their parents. The last stage of change is when the froglets lose their fishy tails.

sink, but a substance that surrounds them swells up to form a jelly. The jelly lifts the eggs to the surface of the water where they float until they hatch. It also tastes bad so the eggs are protected from predators.

Most frogs and toads pay no attention to their offspring once the eggs have been laid, but a few frogs are conscientious parents.

▼ Frogs gather in freshwater pools to mate. The male African bullfrog in this picture has four females to choose from. Male frogs that cannot find a mate will grasp on to other males, floating logs or passing fish!

EGG MINDERS

The male midwife toad wraps the eggs he has fertilised around the back of his body. He keeps them with him until they are ready to hatch.

Great grey tree frogs make a foam nest for their eggs. The nests are made on branches overhanging pools and streams.

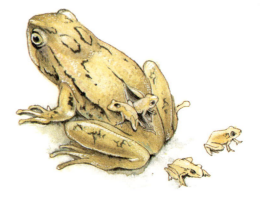

The marsupial tree frog keeps her newly fertilised eggs in a pouch on her back. After a few weeks, she releases tiny froglets from the pouch.

MATING TIME

Most frogs begin life in freshwater pools. As adults, they return to the water to mate and lay eggs. Sometimes frogs instinctively return to the pool of their birth even if it has dried up or been covered over.

The male frogs arrive at the breeding ponds first and call to attract their mates. When the female frogs arrive, there is a lot of activity as frogs compete to secure a partner.

Male frogs choose their mates by jumping on a female's back and gripping her under the forelegs or around the waist. Male frogs have rough pads on their thumbs to help them keep hold of their partners.

Mating frogs may stay entwined for hours or days before the female lays her eggs. As soon as the eggs appear in the water, they are fertilised by the male frog's sperm. Some female frogs can lay over 5,000 eggs in a season.

As frog's eggs enter the water they

▶ Frogs rarely stray far from the freshwater pools they were born in. In fact, a few frogs stay in water all their lives. Frogs can breathe with lungs like people or use internal gills like fish. They can also take in oxygen through their skin. This is the golden bell frog from New Zealand.

◀ Some of the most beautiful frogs live in warm, damp rainforest. They spend their time in the forest canopy. Tree frogs have tiny suckers on the tips of their toes to help them climb rainforest trees.

▲ Some frogs, like the African bullfrog shown here, like to burrow underground. They shuffle backwards into the mud. Frogs that hibernate during the winter bury themselves completely and manage to survive by taking in oxygen through their skin.

FROG TALK

Frogs can be very noisy animals, especially during their breeding season. Some frogs croak, others whistle or make a high-pitched piping noise. Bullfrogs are famed for their loud, bull-like bellows. Many frogs have one or two vocal sacs which they inflate with air to make their calls sound louder.

HOMES FOR FROGS

Frogs live all over the world. There is only one continent where they cannot survive and that is the frozen landmass called Antarctica.

Frogs can be found in many different habitats, from the top of forest trees to the bottom of muddy burrows. They need fresh water to breed so many frogs live near lakes, rivers, ponds or streams.

Because of their moist skin, most frogs need a humid environment. Without damp air, their skin quickly dries up. However, a few frogs have learned to survive in deserts and only mate after rare rainstorms.

Frogs are cold-blooded. This does not mean that their blood is cold. It means they cannot maintain their body temperature. They are affected by the temperature of their environment, so must avoid extreme hot or cold.

In cool climates, frogs hibernate during the winter. They burrow underground or bury themselves in mud at the bottom of their local pond. Desert frogs hide underground too, to avoid the hot and cold parts of the day.